50 Essential Cookbook Recipes

By: Kelly Johnson

Table of Contents

- Classic Beef Stew
- Roasted Chicken
- Spaghetti Bolognese
- Chicken Pot Pie
- Pancakes
- Beef Tacos
- Grilled Cheese Sandwich
- Caesar Salad
- Meatloaf
- Chicken Alfredo
- Shrimp Scampi
- Homemade Pizza Dough
- Quiche Lorraine
- Chicken Curry
- Risotto
- Grilled Salmon
- Roasted Vegetables
- Chicken Caesar Wraps
- Spaghetti Carbonara
- Vegetable Stir-fry
- Shepherd's Pie
- BBQ Ribs
- Egg Salad
- Sloppy Joes
- Beef and Broccoli Stir-fry
- Fettuccine Alfredo
- Beef Enchiladas
- Chicken and Rice Casserole
- Chili
- Tuna Salad
- Chicken Marsala
- Grilled Steak
- Fried Rice
- Chicken Schnitzel
- Stuffed Bell Peppers

- Pad Thai
- Grilled Shrimp Skewers
- Beef Wellington
- Crab Cakes
- Sweet and Sour Chicken
- Lasagna
- Beef Burritos
- Shrimp Tacos
- Ratatouille
- Fish Tacos
- Macaroni and Cheese
- Beef Tacos
- Chicken Fajitas
- Spaghetti and Meatballs
- Potato Gratin

Classic Beef Stew

Ingredients:

- 2 lbs beef stew meat, cubed
- 3 tablespoons vegetable oil
- 1 large onion, chopped
- 2 cloves garlic, minced
- 4 cups beef broth
- 4 medium potatoes, peeled and diced
- 3 carrots, peeled and sliced
- 2 celery stalks, chopped
- 2 tablespoons tomato paste
- 1 teaspoon dried thyme
- 1 teaspoon dried rosemary
- Salt and pepper to taste
- 1 cup frozen peas
- 2 tablespoons cornstarch (optional for thickening)

Instructions:

1. Heat the vegetable oil in a large pot over medium heat. Brown the beef stew meat in batches, then remove and set aside.
2. In the same pot, sauté onion and garlic until soft. Add tomato paste and cook for 2 minutes.
3. Return the beef to the pot, then add beef broth, potatoes, carrots, celery, thyme, rosemary, salt, and pepper. Bring to a boil.
4. Reduce the heat to low, cover, and simmer for 1.5 to 2 hours, or until the beef is tender.
5. If you prefer a thicker stew, mix cornstarch with water and stir it into the stew. Let it simmer for an additional 10 minutes.
6. Stir in the peas and cook for another 5 minutes. Serve hot.

Roasted Chicken

Ingredients:

- 1 whole chicken (3-4 lbs)
- 3 tablespoons olive oil
- 1 lemon, halved
- 4 garlic cloves, smashed
- 1 onion, quartered
- 2 sprigs rosemary
- 1 teaspoon salt
- 1/2 teaspoon black pepper
- 1/2 teaspoon paprika

Instructions:

1. Preheat the oven to 425°F (220°C).
2. Pat the chicken dry with paper towels. Rub the chicken with olive oil and season it with salt, pepper, and paprika.
3. Stuff the chicken cavity with lemon halves, garlic, onion, and rosemary.
4. Place the chicken in a roasting pan, breast-side up, and roast for 1 hour and 15 minutes, or until the internal temperature reaches 165°F (75°C).
5. Let the chicken rest for 10 minutes before carving. Serve with roasted vegetables or potatoes.

Spaghetti Bolognese

Ingredients:

- 1 lb ground beef
- 1 medium onion, chopped
- 2 cloves garlic, minced
- 1 carrot, finely chopped
- 1 celery stalk, chopped
- 1 can (14 oz) crushed tomatoes
- 1/4 cup red wine (optional)
- 1 tablespoon tomato paste
- 1 teaspoon dried oregano
- 1 teaspoon dried basil
- Salt and pepper to taste
- 1/2 cup whole milk or cream
- 1 lb spaghetti
- Fresh parsley (for garnish)

Instructions:

1. In a large skillet, cook ground beef over medium heat until browned. Remove excess fat.
2. Add onion, garlic, carrot, and celery. Cook until softened, about 5 minutes.
3. Stir in crushed tomatoes, tomato paste, red wine (if using), oregano, basil, salt, and pepper. Simmer for 30 minutes, stirring occasionally.
4. Stir in milk or cream and cook for an additional 5 minutes.
5. While the sauce is simmering, cook spaghetti according to package instructions. Drain and set aside.
6. Serve the Bolognese sauce over spaghetti and garnish with fresh parsley.

Chicken Pot Pie

Ingredients:

- 2 cups cooked chicken, shredded
- 1 cup frozen peas and carrots
- 1/3 cup butter
- 1/3 cup flour
- 2 1/2 cups chicken broth
- 1/2 cup milk
- Salt and pepper to taste
- 1/2 teaspoon dried thyme
- 1 package refrigerated pie crusts (or homemade)
- 1 egg (for egg wash)

Instructions:

1. Preheat the oven to 400°F (200°C).
2. In a large saucepan, melt butter over medium heat. Stir in flour and cook for 1 minute.
3. Gradually whisk in chicken broth and milk. Cook, stirring constantly, until the mixture thickens.
4. Stir in cooked chicken, peas, carrots, thyme, salt, and pepper. Remove from heat.
5. Unroll one pie crust and fit it into a pie dish. Pour the chicken mixture into the crust.
6. Top with the second pie crust and trim any excess dough. Pinch the edges to seal and cut a few slits in the top for ventilation.
7. Brush the top with a beaten egg.
8. Bake for 30-35 minutes, or until the crust is golden brown. Let it cool for a few minutes before serving.

Pancakes

Ingredients:

- 1 1/2 cups all-purpose flour
- 3 1/2 teaspoons baking powder
- 1 tablespoon sugar
- 1/2 teaspoon salt
- 1 1/4 cups milk
- 1 large egg
- 3 tablespoons melted butter
- 1 teaspoon vanilla extract

Instructions:

1. In a large bowl, whisk together flour, baking powder, sugar, and salt.
2. In a separate bowl, beat together milk, egg, melted butter, and vanilla extract.
3. Pour the wet ingredients into the dry ingredients and stir until just combined (lumps are okay).
4. Heat a skillet or griddle over medium heat and lightly grease with butter or cooking spray.
5. Pour 1/4 cup of batter onto the skillet for each pancake. Cook until bubbles form on the surface, then flip and cook for an additional 1-2 minutes.
6. Serve with maple syrup and your favorite toppings.

Beef Tacos

Ingredients:

- 1 lb ground beef
- 1 small onion, chopped
- 1 packet taco seasoning
- 1/2 cup water
- 8 small taco shells
- Toppings: shredded lettuce, diced tomatoes, shredded cheese, sour cream, salsa, etc.

Instructions:

1. In a large skillet, cook ground beef and onion over medium heat until the beef is browned.
2. Stir in taco seasoning and water. Simmer for 5-10 minutes, or until the sauce thickens.
3. Warm the taco shells according to package instructions.
4. Spoon the beef mixture into the taco shells and add your desired toppings.
5. Serve immediately.

Grilled Cheese Sandwich

Ingredients:

- 2 slices bread
- 2 slices cheese (American, cheddar, or your choice)
- 1 tablespoon butter

Instructions:

1. Heat a skillet over medium heat.
2. Butter one side of each slice of bread.
3. Place one slice of bread, butter side down, in the skillet. Top with cheese and the second slice of bread, butter side up.
4. Grill for 2-3 minutes per side, or until golden brown and the cheese is melted.
5. Serve hot.

Caesar Salad

Ingredients:

- 4 cups romaine lettuce, chopped
- 1/2 cup Caesar dressing
- 1/4 cup grated Parmesan cheese
- 1/2 cup croutons
- Freshly ground black pepper (optional)

Instructions:

1. In a large bowl, toss the lettuce with Caesar dressing until evenly coated.
2. Add Parmesan cheese and croutons. Toss gently.
3. Top with freshly ground black pepper, if desired.
4. Serve immediately.

Meatloaf

Ingredients:

- 1 lb ground beef
- 1/2 lb ground pork
- 1 small onion, chopped
- 1 clove garlic, minced
- 1/2 cup breadcrumbs
- 1/4 cup milk
- 1 large egg
- 1/4 cup ketchup
- 1 tablespoon Worcestershire sauce
- Salt and pepper to taste
- 1/4 cup ketchup (for topping)

Instructions:

1. Preheat the oven to 350°F (175°C).
2. In a large bowl, combine ground beef, ground pork, onion, garlic, breadcrumbs, milk, egg, ketchup, Worcestershire sauce, salt, and pepper. Mix well.
3. Form the mixture into a loaf shape and place in a greased baking dish.
4. Spread the remaining ketchup on top of the meatloaf.
5. Bake for 60-70 minutes, or until the meatloaf reaches an internal temperature of 160°F (71°C).
6. Let it rest for 10 minutes before slicing and serving.

Chicken Alfredo

Ingredients:

- 1 lb fettuccine pasta
- 2 tablespoons olive oil
- 2 chicken breasts, boneless and skinless
- Salt and pepper to taste
- 1/2 cup heavy cream
- 1/2 cup grated Parmesan cheese
- 2 cloves garlic, minced
- 2 tablespoons unsalted butter
- Fresh parsley (for garnish)

Instructions:

1. Cook fettuccine according to package instructions. Drain and set aside.
2. Heat olive oil in a skillet over medium heat. Season chicken breasts with salt and pepper, then cook for 6-7 minutes per side, or until cooked through. Slice the chicken into thin strips.
3. In the same skillet, melt butter over medium heat. Add garlic and cook for 1 minute.
4. Add heavy cream and bring to a simmer. Stir in Parmesan cheese and cook for 3-4 minutes, or until the sauce thickens.
5. Add the cooked pasta and sliced chicken to the skillet, tossing to coat in the sauce.
6. Garnish with fresh parsley and serve.

Shrimp Scampi

Ingredients:

- 1 lb large shrimp, peeled and deveined
- 8 oz linguine or spaghetti
- 3 tablespoons butter
- 3 tablespoons olive oil
- 4 cloves garlic, minced
- 1/2 cup dry white wine
- 1/2 teaspoon red pepper flakes (optional)
- Salt and pepper to taste
- Fresh parsley, chopped (for garnish)
- Lemon wedges (for serving)

Instructions:

1. Cook linguine or spaghetti according to package instructions. Drain and set aside.
2. In a large skillet, melt butter and olive oil over medium heat. Add garlic and cook for 1 minute, until fragrant.
3. Add shrimp and cook for 2-3 minutes per side, or until pink and cooked through. Remove shrimp from the skillet.
4. Add white wine to the skillet and bring to a simmer. Cook for 2 minutes to reduce slightly.
5. Return the shrimp to the skillet, add red pepper flakes (if using), and toss with the pasta.
6. Season with salt and pepper. Garnish with parsley and serve with lemon wedges.

Homemade Pizza Dough

Ingredients:

- 2 1/4 teaspoons active dry yeast
- 1 teaspoon sugar
- 1 1/2 cups warm water
- 3 1/2 cups all-purpose flour
- 2 tablespoons olive oil
- 1 teaspoon salt

Instructions:

1. In a small bowl, dissolve yeast and sugar in warm water. Let it sit for 5 minutes, until frothy.
2. In a large bowl, combine flour, olive oil, and salt. Add the yeast mixture and stir to form a dough.
3. Knead the dough on a lightly floured surface for 8-10 minutes, or until smooth.
4. Place the dough in a greased bowl, cover with a cloth, and let it rise for 1-2 hours, or until doubled in size.
5. Preheat your oven to 475°F (245°C). Punch down the dough and divide it in half for two pizza crusts.
6. Roll out the dough and add your desired toppings before baking for 10-12 minutes.

Quiche Lorraine

Ingredients:

- 1 pie crust (store-bought or homemade)
- 6 large eggs
- 1 cup heavy cream
- 1 cup milk
- 1/2 teaspoon salt
- 1/4 teaspoon black pepper
- 1/2 teaspoon nutmeg (optional)
- 1 cup cooked bacon, chopped
- 1/2 cup grated Gruyère cheese
- 1/2 cup chopped onions (optional)

Instructions:

1. Preheat oven to 375°F (190°C).
2. In a bowl, whisk together eggs, cream, milk, salt, pepper, and nutmeg.
3. Place the pie crust in a pie dish and layer the cooked bacon, cheese, and onions in the bottom.
4. Pour the egg mixture over the filling.
5. Bake for 40-45 minutes, or until the quiche is set and the top is golden brown.
6. Let cool for 10 minutes before slicing and serving.

Chicken Curry

Ingredients:

- 1 lb chicken breasts, cut into chunks
- 1 tablespoon olive oil
- 1 onion, chopped
- 2 cloves garlic, minced
- 1 tablespoon grated ginger
- 1 tablespoon curry powder
- 1 teaspoon turmeric
- 1 teaspoon cumin
- 1 can (14 oz) coconut milk
- 1 cup chicken broth
- 1 cup diced tomatoes
- Salt and pepper to taste
- Fresh cilantro, chopped (optional)

Instructions:

1. Heat olive oil in a large pot over medium heat. Add the onions, garlic, and ginger and sauté for 3-4 minutes until softened.
2. Add the curry powder, turmeric, and cumin, and cook for another 1-2 minutes to release the spices' aroma.
3. Add the chicken chunks and cook until browned on all sides, about 5-7 minutes.
4. Stir in the coconut milk, chicken broth, and diced tomatoes. Bring to a simmer and cook for 20-25 minutes, until the chicken is fully cooked and the sauce thickens.
5. Season with salt and pepper, and garnish with fresh cilantro before serving.

Risotto

Ingredients:

- 1 1/2 cups Arborio rice
- 4 cups chicken or vegetable broth, kept warm
- 1/2 cup dry white wine
- 1 tablespoon olive oil
- 1 small onion, chopped
- 2 cloves garlic, minced
- 1/2 cup grated Parmesan cheese
- 2 tablespoons unsalted butter
- Salt and pepper to taste

Instructions:

1. Heat olive oil in a large pan over medium heat. Add the onion and garlic, and sauté for 3-4 minutes until softened.
2. Add the Arborio rice and cook, stirring constantly, for 2 minutes to lightly toast the rice.
3. Add the white wine and cook until it's mostly absorbed by the rice.
4. Begin adding the warm broth, one ladleful at a time, stirring constantly and letting the rice absorb the liquid before adding more.
5. Continue this process for about 18-20 minutes, until the rice is creamy and cooked through.
6. Stir in the butter and Parmesan cheese, and season with salt and pepper to taste before serving.

Grilled Salmon

Ingredients:

- 4 salmon fillets
- 2 tablespoons olive oil
- 1 lemon, sliced
- 2 cloves garlic, minced
- 1 teaspoon dried thyme
- Salt and pepper to taste

Instructions:

1. Preheat grill to medium-high heat.
2. Brush the salmon fillets with olive oil, and season with garlic, thyme, salt, and pepper.
3. Place the salmon on the grill, skin-side down, and cook for 4-5 minutes per side, until the salmon is cooked through and flakes easily with a fork.
4. Serve with lemon slices on the side.

Roasted Vegetables

Ingredients:

- 2 cups carrots, peeled and sliced
- 2 cups broccoli florets
- 1 red bell pepper, chopped
- 1 zucchini, sliced
- 2 tablespoons olive oil
- 1 teaspoon dried thyme
- Salt and pepper to taste

Instructions:

1. Preheat oven to 400°F (200°C).
2. In a large bowl, toss all vegetables with olive oil, thyme, salt, and pepper.
3. Spread the vegetables in a single layer on a baking sheet.
4. Roast for 20-25 minutes, stirring once, until the vegetables are tender and lightly browned.

Chicken Caesar Wraps

Ingredients:

- 2 cups cooked chicken breast, sliced
- 1 cup romaine lettuce, chopped
- 1/2 cup Caesar dressing
- 1/4 cup grated Parmesan cheese
- 4 large flour tortillas

Instructions:

1. In a bowl, toss the chicken, lettuce, Caesar dressing, and Parmesan cheese.
2. Lay the tortillas flat and divide the chicken mixture among them.
3. Fold in the sides and roll up the tortillas into wraps.
4. Serve immediately or wrap in foil for an easy on-the-go meal.

Spaghetti Carbonara

Ingredients:

- 8 oz spaghetti
- 4 oz pancetta or bacon, diced
- 2 large eggs
- 1/2 cup grated Parmesan cheese
- 1/4 cup heavy cream
- 2 cloves garlic, minced
- Salt and pepper to taste

Instructions:

1. Cook spaghetti according to package instructions. Drain, reserving some pasta water.
2. In a large skillet, cook pancetta or bacon over medium heat until crispy, about 5-7 minutes.
3. In a bowl, whisk together eggs, Parmesan, heavy cream, salt, and pepper.
4. Add the cooked spaghetti to the skillet with pancetta, and toss to coat. Remove from heat and quickly stir in the egg mixture, adding pasta water as needed to create a creamy sauce.
5. Serve with extra Parmesan and freshly ground black pepper.

Vegetable Stir-fry

Ingredients:

- 1 cup broccoli florets
- 1 red bell pepper, sliced
- 1 carrot, julienned
- 1/2 onion, sliced
- 2 tablespoons soy sauce
- 1 tablespoon sesame oil
- 1 tablespoon olive oil
- 1 teaspoon ginger, minced
- 2 cloves garlic, minced

Instructions:

1. Heat olive oil in a large skillet or wok over medium-high heat.
2. Add the broccoli, bell pepper, carrot, and onion. Stir-fry for 5-7 minutes, until the vegetables are tender-crisp.
3. Add garlic and ginger and cook for another minute.
4. Stir in soy sauce and sesame oil, and toss to coat.
5. Serve immediately with steamed rice or noodles.

Shepherd's Pie

Ingredients:

- 1 lb ground lamb or beef
- 1 onion, chopped
- 2 carrots, diced
- 1 cup peas
- 1 cup beef broth
- 2 tablespoons tomato paste
- 2 teaspoons Worcestershire sauce
- 4 cups mashed potatoes
- Salt and pepper to taste

Instructions:

1. Preheat oven to 375°F (190°C).
2. In a large skillet, cook the ground lamb or beef with the onion and carrots until browned.
3. Stir in peas, beef broth, tomato paste, Worcestershire sauce, salt, and pepper. Simmer for 5-10 minutes until the mixture thickens.
4. Transfer the meat mixture to a baking dish and top with mashed potatoes, spreading evenly.
5. Bake for 20 minutes, until the top is golden brown.
6. Serve hot.

BBQ Ribs

Ingredients:

- 2 racks of baby back ribs
- 1/2 cup BBQ sauce
- Salt and pepper to taste
- 1 tablespoon olive oil

Instructions:

1. Preheat oven to 300°F (150°C).
2. Season the ribs with salt, pepper, and olive oil.
3. Place the ribs on a baking sheet, cover with foil, and bake for 2-2.5 hours.
4. Preheat a grill to medium heat. Transfer the ribs to the grill and brush with BBQ sauce.
5. Grill for 5-7 minutes per side, brushing with more sauce as needed.
6. Serve hot.

Egg Salad

Ingredients:

- 6 large eggs, boiled and chopped
- 1/4 cup mayonnaise
- 1 tablespoon Dijon mustard
- 1 teaspoon vinegar
- 1 tablespoon chives, chopped
- Salt and pepper to taste

Instructions:

1. In a bowl, mix the boiled eggs with mayonnaise, mustard, vinegar, chives, salt, and pepper.
2. Stir until well combined. Serve on toast, in a sandwich, or as a salad topping.

Sloppy Joes

Ingredients:

- 1 lb ground beef
- 1 small onion, chopped
- 1/2 green bell pepper, chopped
- 2 cloves garlic, minced
- 1 cup ketchup
- 1 tablespoon Worcestershire sauce
- 1 tablespoon brown sugar
- 1 teaspoon mustard
- Salt and pepper to taste
- 4 hamburger buns

Instructions:

1. In a large skillet, cook the ground beef over medium heat until browned. Drain excess fat.
2. Add the onion, bell pepper, and garlic. Cook until softened, about 5 minutes.
3. Stir in ketchup, Worcestershire sauce, brown sugar, mustard, salt, and pepper. Simmer for 10 minutes, stirring occasionally.
4. Serve the mixture on hamburger buns and enjoy!

Beef and Broccoli Stir-fry

Ingredients:

- 1 lb flank steak, thinly sliced
- 2 cups broccoli florets
- 2 tablespoons soy sauce
- 2 tablespoons oyster sauce
- 1 tablespoon hoisin sauce
- 1 tablespoon sesame oil
- 2 cloves garlic, minced
- 1 tablespoon cornstarch mixed with 2 tablespoons water
- 1 tablespoon vegetable oil

Instructions:

1. Heat vegetable oil in a large skillet or wok over medium-high heat. Add the beef and cook until browned, about 3-5 minutes.

2. Remove the beef and set aside. In the same skillet, add garlic and cook for 30 seconds until fragrant.
3. Add the broccoli and stir-fry for 3-4 minutes, until tender-crisp.
4. Stir in soy sauce, oyster sauce, hoisin sauce, and sesame oil. Add the beef back into the skillet and toss to coat.
5. Stir in the cornstarch mixture and cook for 1-2 minutes until the sauce thickens. Serve with rice.

Fettuccine Alfredo

Ingredients:

- 12 oz fettuccine pasta
- 1 cup heavy cream
- 1/2 cup unsalted butter
- 2 cloves garlic, minced
- 1 cup grated Parmesan cheese
- Salt and pepper to taste
- Fresh parsley (for garnish)

Instructions:

1. Cook fettuccine pasta according to package directions. Drain and set aside.
2. In a large skillet, melt butter over medium heat. Add garlic and cook for 1-2 minutes until fragrant.
3. Stir in the heavy cream and bring to a simmer. Cook for 3-4 minutes, stirring occasionally.
4. Add Parmesan cheese and stir until the sauce thickens. Season with salt and pepper.
5. Toss the cooked pasta with the sauce and serve with fresh parsley.

Beef Enchiladas

Ingredients:

- 1 lb ground beef
- 1 small onion, chopped
- 1 packet enchilada seasoning
- 1 can (10 oz) red enchilada sauce
- 8 flour tortillas
- 2 cups shredded cheddar cheese
- 1 cup sour cream (optional)
- Fresh cilantro (for garnish)

Instructions:

1. Preheat oven to 375°F (190°C).
2. In a skillet, cook ground beef and onion over medium heat until browned. Drain excess fat.
3. Stir in the enchilada seasoning and half of the enchilada sauce. Simmer for 5 minutes.
4. Warm the tortillas and spoon the beef mixture onto each tortilla. Roll up and place seam-side down in a baking dish.
5. Pour the remaining enchilada sauce over the top and sprinkle with shredded cheese.
6. Bake for 20 minutes, or until the cheese is melted and bubbly.
7. Serve with sour cream and fresh cilantro.

Chicken and Rice Casserole

Ingredients:

- 2 cups cooked chicken, shredded
- 1 cup long-grain white rice
- 1 can (10.5 oz) cream of chicken soup
- 1 cup chicken broth
- 1 cup shredded cheddar cheese
- 1/2 cup frozen peas
- Salt and pepper to taste

Instructions:

1. Preheat oven to 375°F (190°C).
2. In a large mixing bowl, combine shredded chicken, cooked rice, cream of chicken soup, chicken broth, peas, salt, and pepper.
3. Transfer the mixture to a greased baking dish and top with shredded cheese.
4. Cover with foil and bake for 25 minutes. Remove foil and bake for an additional 10 minutes until the cheese is golden and bubbly.

Chili

Ingredients:

- 1 lb ground beef
- 1 onion, chopped
- 2 cloves garlic, minced
- 1 can (15 oz) kidney beans, drained
- 1 can (15 oz) diced tomatoes
- 1 can (6 oz) tomato paste
- 1 packet chili seasoning mix
- 1/2 cup beef broth
- Salt and pepper to taste
- Optional toppings: sour cream, shredded cheese, green onions

Instructions:

1. In a large pot, brown the ground beef over medium heat. Drain excess fat.
2. Add the onion and garlic, cooking until softened, about 5 minutes.
3. Stir in beans, diced tomatoes, tomato paste, chili seasoning, and beef broth. Bring to a boil, then reduce heat and simmer for 30 minutes.
4. Season with salt and pepper and serve with desired toppings.

Tuna Salad

Ingredients:

- 2 cans (5 oz each) tuna, drained
- 1/2 cup mayonnaise
- 1 tablespoon Dijon mustard
- 1 tablespoon relish (optional)
- 1/2 small onion, chopped
- Salt and pepper to taste
- Fresh parsley (optional)

Instructions:

1. In a medium bowl, combine tuna, mayonnaise, mustard, relish, and onion.
2. Stir until well combined. Season with salt and pepper.
3. Garnish with fresh parsley if desired. Serve on bread, crackers, or a bed of greens.

Chicken Marsala

Ingredients:

- 4 boneless, skinless chicken breasts
- 1/2 cup flour
- 2 tablespoons olive oil
- 1 cup Marsala wine
- 1 cup chicken broth
- 1 cup mushrooms, sliced
- 1 tablespoon butter
- Salt and pepper to taste
- Fresh parsley (for garnish)

Instructions:

1. Coat chicken breasts in flour, shaking off excess.
2. Heat olive oil in a large skillet over medium-high heat. Cook the chicken for 5-6 minutes per side, until browned and cooked through. Remove and set aside.
3. In the same skillet, add mushrooms and cook for 3-4 minutes until soft.
4. Stir in Marsala wine and chicken broth, scraping up any browned bits from the bottom of the skillet. Bring to a simmer.
5. Return the chicken to the skillet and cook for 5 minutes until the sauce thickens.
6. Stir in butter, season with salt and pepper, and garnish with parsley before serving.

Grilled Steak

Ingredients:

- 2 rib-eye steaks (or preferred cut)
- 2 tablespoons olive oil
- 1 teaspoon garlic powder
- Salt and pepper to taste
- Fresh thyme or rosemary (optional)

Instructions:

1. Preheat grill to medium-high heat.
2. Rub the steaks with olive oil and season with garlic powder, salt, and pepper.
3. Grill steaks for 4-5 minutes per side, or to your desired level of doneness.
4. Remove from the grill and let rest for 5 minutes before serving. Garnish with fresh herbs if desired.

Fried Rice

Ingredients:

- 2 cups cooked rice (preferably chilled)
- 2 tablespoons vegetable oil
- 2 eggs, scrambled
- 1 small onion, chopped
- 1/2 cup frozen peas and carrots
- 2 tablespoons soy sauce
- 1 teaspoon sesame oil
- Green onions for garnish

Instructions:

1. Heat vegetable oil in a large skillet or wok over medium-high heat. Add the onion and cook until softened, about 3 minutes.
2. Add peas and carrots and cook for an additional 2 minutes.
3. Push vegetables to the side of the skillet and scramble eggs on the other side until cooked through.
4. Add rice to the skillet and stir to combine. Add soy sauce and sesame oil, cooking for another 3-4 minutes.
5. Garnish with green onions and serve.

Chicken Schnitzel

Ingredients:

- 4 boneless, skinless chicken breasts
- 1/2 cup all-purpose flour
- 2 eggs, beaten
- 1 cup breadcrumbs
- 1 teaspoon salt
- 1 teaspoon pepper
- 1 teaspoon paprika
- 1/4 cup vegetable oil
- Lemon wedges for serving

Instructions:

1. Flatten the chicken breasts to even thickness by pounding them between two sheets of plastic wrap.
2. Dredge the chicken in flour, dip in beaten eggs, and coat with breadcrumbs.
3. Heat vegetable oil in a large skillet over medium-high heat. Cook the chicken for 3-4 minutes per side, until golden brown and cooked through.
4. Remove from the skillet and serve with lemon wedges.

Stuffed Bell Peppers

Ingredients:

- 4 bell peppers, tops cut off and seeds removed
- 1 lb ground beef or turkey
- 1 small onion, chopped
- 2 cloves garlic, minced
- 1 cup cooked rice
- 1 can (14.5 oz) diced tomatoes
- 1 tablespoon tomato paste
- 1 teaspoon dried oregano
- 1 teaspoon paprika
- 1 cup shredded cheese (cheddar or mozzarella)
- Salt and pepper to taste

Instructions:

1. Preheat oven to 375°F (190°C).
2. In a skillet, cook the ground beef or turkey with onion and garlic over medium heat until browned. Drain excess fat.
3. Stir in diced tomatoes, tomato paste, oregano, paprika, rice, salt, and pepper. Simmer for 5 minutes.
4. Stuff the peppers with the mixture and place them in a baking dish.
5. Top with shredded cheese and bake for 30 minutes until peppers are tender and cheese is melted.

Pad Thai

Ingredients:

- 8 oz rice noodles
- 2 tablespoons vegetable oil
- 2 eggs, lightly beaten
- 1 cup shrimp, chicken, or tofu (optional)
- 2 cloves garlic, minced
- 1/2 cup shredded carrots
- 1/4 cup chopped green onions
- 1/4 cup roasted peanuts, chopped
- 1 lime, cut into wedges
- 2 tablespoons soy sauce
- 1 tablespoon fish sauce
- 1 tablespoon brown sugar
- 1 tablespoon rice vinegar
- 1 teaspoon chili flakes (optional)

Instructions:

1. Cook rice noodles according to package instructions, drain and set aside.
2. In a large pan, heat vegetable oil over medium-high heat. Scramble the eggs in the pan until cooked through, then set aside.
3. In the same pan, add shrimp or chicken (if using) and cook until fully cooked.
4. Add garlic and carrots, cooking for 1-2 minutes.
5. Stir in the cooked noodles, soy sauce, fish sauce, brown sugar, rice vinegar, and chili flakes. Toss to combine.
6. Add scrambled eggs and green onions, tossing again. Serve with chopped peanuts and lime wedges.

Grilled Shrimp Skewers

Ingredients:

- 1 lb shrimp, peeled and deveined
- 2 tablespoons olive oil
- 2 cloves garlic, minced
- 1 teaspoon smoked paprika
- 1 teaspoon lemon zest
- 1 tablespoon lemon juice
- Salt and pepper to taste
- Wooden or metal skewers

Instructions:

1. Preheat grill to medium-high heat.
2. In a bowl, toss the shrimp with olive oil, garlic, paprika, lemon zest, lemon juice, salt, and pepper.
3. Thread the shrimp onto skewers.
4. Grill the shrimp for 2-3 minutes per side, or until pink and cooked through.
5. Serve immediately with extra lemon wedges.

Beef Wellington

Ingredients:

- 1.5 lb beef tenderloin, trimmed
- 2 tablespoons olive oil
- 1/2 lb mushrooms, finely chopped
- 2 tablespoons Dijon mustard
- 2 tablespoons unsalted butter
- 1/2 cup prosciutto, sliced thin
- 1 sheet puff pastry
- 1 egg, beaten
- Salt and pepper to taste

Instructions:

1. Preheat oven to 400°F (200°C).
2. Sear the beef tenderloin in olive oil on all sides over high heat. Remove from heat and brush with Dijon mustard. Let cool.
3. In a skillet, melt butter and sauté mushrooms until all moisture evaporates, about 5-7 minutes. Season with salt and pepper.
4. Lay prosciutto slices on plastic wrap, spread mushroom mixture on top, and place beef in the center. Roll up tightly and refrigerate for 30 minutes.
5. Roll out puff pastry and place the beef in the center. Wrap the beef tightly in the pastry and seal the edges.
6. Brush with beaten egg and bake for 25-30 minutes, or until golden brown and the internal temperature reaches 125°F (for medium-rare).
7. Let rest before slicing and serving.

Crab Cakes

Ingredients:

- 1 lb crab meat, drained and picked over
- 1/2 cup breadcrumbs
- 1/4 cup mayonnaise
- 1 tablespoon Dijon mustard
- 1 egg, beaten
- 1 tablespoon Old Bay seasoning
- 1/4 cup chopped green onions
- 2 tablespoons parsley, chopped
- Vegetable oil for frying

Instructions:

1. In a bowl, combine crab meat, breadcrumbs, mayonnaise, mustard, egg, Old Bay seasoning, green onions, and parsley. Gently mix until combined.
2. Form the mixture into patties, about 3 inches in diameter.
3. Heat oil in a skillet over medium heat. Cook the crab cakes for 4-5 minutes per side, or until golden brown.
4. Serve with tartar sauce or a squeeze of lemon.

Sweet and Sour Chicken

Ingredients:

- 1 lb chicken breast, cut into bite-sized pieces
- 1/2 cup cornstarch
- 1 egg, beaten
- 2 tablespoons vegetable oil
- 1/2 cup vinegar
- 1/4 cup sugar
- 1/4 cup ketchup
- 2 tablespoons soy sauce
- 1 red bell pepper, chopped
- 1/2 onion, chopped
- 1/2 cup pineapple chunks

Instructions:

1. Dredge chicken pieces in cornstarch, then dip in beaten egg.
2. Heat vegetable oil in a large skillet over medium heat. Fry chicken in batches until golden brown, about 5 minutes per batch.
3. In a separate pan, combine vinegar, sugar, ketchup, soy sauce, bell pepper, onion, and pineapple. Bring to a boil, then simmer for 5-7 minutes.
4. Toss the fried chicken in the sweet and sour sauce until coated. Serve with rice.

Lasagna

Ingredients:

- 12 lasagna noodles, cooked and drained
- 1 lb ground beef
- 1 onion, chopped
- 2 cloves garlic, minced
- 1 jar (24 oz) marinara sauce
- 1 can (6 oz) tomato paste
- 15 oz ricotta cheese
- 2 cups shredded mozzarella cheese
- 1/2 cup grated Parmesan cheese
- 1 egg, beaten
- 2 tablespoons fresh basil, chopped

Instructions:

1. Preheat oven to 375°F (190°C).
2. In a skillet, cook ground beef, onion, and garlic until browned. Stir in marinara sauce and tomato paste. Simmer for 10 minutes.
3. In a bowl, mix ricotta cheese, mozzarella, Parmesan, egg, and basil.
4. In a baking dish, layer noodles, sauce, and ricotta mixture, repeating until all ingredients are used.
5. Top with remaining mozzarella and bake for 30-35 minutes until bubbly. Let cool for 10 minutes before serving.

Beef Burritos

Ingredients:

- 1 lb ground beef
- 1 packet taco seasoning
- 1 cup cooked rice
- 1 cup shredded cheese (cheddar or Mexican blend)
- 1/2 cup salsa
- 4 large flour tortillas
- Sour cream and guacamole for serving

Instructions:

1. Cook ground beef in a skillet over medium heat until browned. Drain excess fat.
2. Stir in taco seasoning and water as directed on the seasoning packet. Simmer for 5 minutes.
3. Warm tortillas and fill each with beef mixture, rice, cheese, and salsa.
4. Roll up the burritos and serve with sour cream and guacamole.

Shrimp Tacos

Ingredients:

- 1 lb shrimp, peeled and deveined
- 1 tablespoon olive oil
- 1 teaspoon chili powder
- 1 teaspoon cumin
- 1 teaspoon garlic powder
- Salt and pepper to taste
- 8 small corn tortillas
- 1/2 cup shredded cabbage
- 1/4 cup cilantro, chopped
- 1 lime, cut into wedges
- 1/4 cup sour cream

Instructions:

1. In a bowl, toss shrimp with olive oil, chili powder, cumin, garlic powder, salt, and pepper.
2. Heat a skillet over medium-high heat and cook shrimp for 2-3 minutes per side, until pink.
3. Warm tortillas and assemble tacos with shrimp, cabbage, cilantro, and a squeeze of lime. Top with sour cream.

Ratatouille

Ingredients:

- 1 eggplant, chopped
- 1 zucchini, chopped
- 1 red bell pepper, chopped
- 1 yellow onion, chopped
- 2 cloves garlic, minced
- 2 cups diced tomatoes
- 2 tablespoons olive oil
- 1 teaspoon dried thyme
- Salt and pepper to taste
- Fresh basil for garnish

Instructions:

1. Heat olive oil in a large skillet over medium heat. Add onion and garlic, cooking until softened.
2. Add eggplant, zucchini, and bell pepper. Cook for 5-7 minutes, stirring occasionally.
3. Stir in diced tomatoes, thyme, salt, and pepper. Simmer for 10 minutes, until vegetables are tender.
4. Garnish with fresh basil and serve.

Fish Tacos

Ingredients:

- 1 lb white fish fillets (such as cod or tilapia)
- 1 tablespoon olive oil
- 1 teaspoon chili powder
- 1 teaspoon cumin
- 1/2 teaspoon garlic powder
- Salt and pepper to taste
- 8 small corn tortillas
- 1/2 cup shredded cabbage
- 1/4 cup cilantro, chopped
- 1 lime, cut into wedges
- 1/4 cup sour cream or crema

Instructions:

1. Preheat oven to 375°F (190°C). Place the fish fillets on a baking sheet and drizzle with olive oil. Season with chili powder, cumin, garlic powder, salt, and pepper.
2. Bake for 10-12 minutes or until the fish is fully cooked and flakes easily with a fork.
3. Warm the tortillas and assemble the tacos with the baked fish, shredded cabbage, cilantro, a squeeze of lime, and a dollop of sour cream.
4. Serve with extra lime wedges.

Macaroni and Cheese

Ingredients:

- 8 oz elbow macaroni
- 2 cups shredded cheddar cheese
- 1/2 cup grated Parmesan cheese
- 1/4 cup unsalted butter
- 2 tablespoons all-purpose flour
- 2 cups milk
- 1/2 teaspoon garlic powder
- Salt and pepper to taste
- 1/4 teaspoon paprika (optional)

Instructions:

1. Cook the macaroni according to package instructions, then drain and set aside.
2. In a large saucepan, melt the butter over medium heat. Add the flour and whisk to create a roux. Cook for 1-2 minutes.
3. Gradually add the milk, whisking continuously until the sauce thickens.
4. Stir in the cheddar cheese, Parmesan, garlic powder, salt, and pepper. Continue stirring until the cheese is melted and smooth.
5. Add the cooked macaroni to the sauce and toss to coat. Serve with a sprinkle of paprika, if desired.

Beef Tacos

Ingredients:

- 1 lb ground beef
- 1 packet taco seasoning (or homemade seasoning)
- 1/4 cup water
- 8 small taco shells (soft or hard)
- Toppings: shredded lettuce, diced tomatoes, shredded cheese, sour cream, salsa, guacamole

Instructions:

1. In a skillet, cook the ground beef over medium heat until browned, breaking it apart as it cooks. Drain any excess fat.
2. Add taco seasoning and water to the beef. Stir and simmer for 5 minutes, until the mixture thickens.
3. Warm taco shells and fill them with the seasoned beef.
4. Add your favorite toppings, such as lettuce, tomatoes, cheese, sour cream, salsa, and guacamole.

Chicken Fajitas

Ingredients:

- 1 lb chicken breasts, sliced into strips
- 1 tablespoon olive oil
- 1 red bell pepper, sliced
- 1 green bell pepper, sliced
- 1 onion, sliced
- 2 teaspoons fajita seasoning
- 1 tablespoon lime juice
- 8 small flour tortillas
- Optional toppings: sour cream, salsa, guacamole, shredded cheese

Instructions:

1. Heat olive oil in a skillet over medium-high heat. Add the chicken strips and cook until browned and cooked through, about 5-7 minutes.
2. Remove the chicken from the pan and add the bell peppers and onion. Cook for 3-4 minutes until softened.
3. Return the chicken to the pan and stir in the fajita seasoning and lime juice. Cook for an additional 2-3 minutes.
4. Warm the tortillas and serve the chicken and vegetables with your favorite toppings.

Spaghetti and Meatballs

Ingredients:

- 8 oz spaghetti
- 1 lb ground beef or a mix of beef and pork
- 1/2 cup breadcrumbs
- 1/4 cup grated Parmesan cheese
- 1 egg
- 2 cloves garlic, minced
- 1 teaspoon dried oregano
- 1 jar (24 oz) marinara sauce
- Fresh basil for garnish (optional)

Instructions:

1. Preheat oven to 375°F (190°C). In a bowl, mix together the ground meat, breadcrumbs, Parmesan cheese, egg, garlic, oregano, salt, and pepper.
2. Form the mixture into meatballs, about 1-2 inches in diameter, and place them on a baking sheet.
3. Bake for 20-25 minutes, or until the meatballs are fully cooked.
4. Meanwhile, cook the spaghetti according to package instructions. Drain and set aside.
5. In a large saucepan, heat the marinara sauce over medium heat. Add the meatballs and simmer for 10 minutes.
6. Serve the meatballs and sauce over spaghetti, garnished with fresh basil if desired.

Potato Gratin

Ingredients:

- 4 large russet potatoes, peeled and thinly sliced
- 2 cups heavy cream
- 1/2 cup milk
- 2 cloves garlic, minced
- 1 1/2 cups shredded Gruyère or cheddar cheese
- Salt and pepper to taste
- Fresh thyme or rosemary for garnish (optional)

Instructions:

1. Preheat oven to 350°F (175°C). Grease a baking dish with butter or cooking spray.
2. In a saucepan, heat the heavy cream, milk, and garlic over medium heat. Once it's hot, remove from heat and season with salt and pepper.
3. Layer the sliced potatoes in the baking dish, slightly overlapping each layer. Pour some of the cream mixture over the potatoes, then sprinkle with cheese.
4. Repeat the layering process until all potatoes and cream mixture are used up, ending with a layer of cheese on top.
5. Cover the dish with foil and bake for 45 minutes. Remove the foil and bake for another 15-20 minutes, until the top is golden brown and the potatoes are tender.
6. Let rest for 10 minutes before serving, and garnish with fresh thyme or rosemary if desired.

www.ingramcontent.com/pod-product-compliance
Lightning Source LLC
LaVergne TN
LVHW081336060526
838201LV00055B/2685